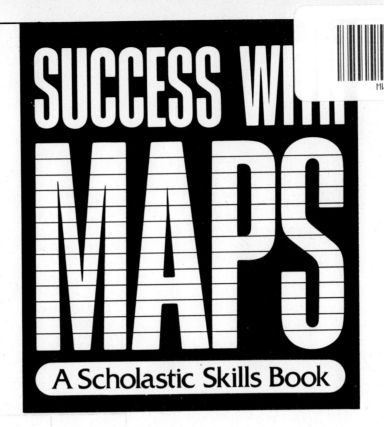

SUCCESS WITH MAPS

A Scholastic Skills Book

by Rebecca Kalusky

SCHOLASTIC INC.

Editor: Mary Lee Johansen
Editorial Director: Eleanor Angeles
Art Director/Designer: Marijka Kostiw

Production Editor: Judy Susman
Consultant: Marjorie Slavick Frank
Cover Illustration: Andrea Baruffi

Photos: 19: *tl* Sybil Shelton/Peter Arnold; *cl* Stephen J. Krasemann/Peter Arnold; *bl* Louis F. Swift; *tr* Lillian N. Bolstad/Peter Arnold; *cr* Amtrak National Railroad Passenger Corp.; *br* Leo de Wys. 21: *t* Leo de Wys. 58: *t* NASA.

Art and Cartography: Eric Barnes: 4; 5; 9; *r* 25; 40; *t* 45; 52. Graphic Chart and Map Company: *b* 21; 27; 29; 31; 36; 37; 39; 46; 47; 49; 51; 54; 55; 57. Andrey Kostiw: 7; 10; 14; *c* 18; 34; 38; 44; 53. Wilhelmina Reyinga: 24; *l* 25; 32; 33; 35; *c* 45; *b* 58–59; 60; 61; 63. S. J. Shue: 6; 8; 11; 12; 13; 15; 16; 50; 56. Mike Suh: *t* 18; 20; 22–23; 26; 30; 41; 42–43.

No part of this publication may be reproduced in whole or in part, or stored in a retrieval system, or transmitted in any form or by any means, electronic, mechanical, photocopying, recording, or otherwise, without written permission of the publisher. For information regarding permission, write to Scholastic Inc., Classroom Magazine Division, 555 Broadway, New York, NY 10012-3999.

ISBN 0-590-34356-4

Copyright © 1985 by Scholastic Inc. All rights reserved. Published by Scholastic Inc.

30 29 28 27 26 25 24 23 22 21   8 9/9 0 1 2 3/0

Printed In the U.S.A.

TABLE OF CONTENTS

PICTURES OF OUR WORLD

Can you answer the riddle?

What can show you . . .

the **names** and shapes of **places** in the world?
how to get from one **place** to **another?**
what direction you are going in?
how far one place is from another?

What's the answer? . . . **MAPS!**

Maps can show you all of that information, and lots more.
Maps are **drawings** of **Earth.** They show what a place would look
like if you were looking down on it. A map can show you the
whole world or just parts of it. This book can help you learn how
to use many different kinds of maps.

Look at the **globe.** Can you find the **United States?**
On the globe, draw a circle around the United States.

First maps

Since early times, people have made **maps.** Even cave people drew maps. Their maps were probably pictures scratched in the ground with a stick. They would show where to find food or where to hunt animals. Here is an example of what one of those maps might have looked like.

The cave people could not write. So there were no **titles** or **labels** on their maps. But you can guess what the pictures stand for.

Follow the directions below. Draw a path to show where you would go if you were a cave person using the map.

1. Start at the cave. Walk past the pond where the tall grass grows. Go to the stream.

2. Walk on the log across the stream.

3. Walk along the stream near the rocks. Go as far as the hill.

4. Walk toward the trees and bushes. You will find animals to hunt and berries to pick.

5. Underline the best title below for the map.

   Walking in the Woods   **Where to Find Food**

A map for today

Here is a **picture map** that people could use today.
There is a **title** to tell you what the map is about. Circle the title.
There are names or **labels** to help you find places.

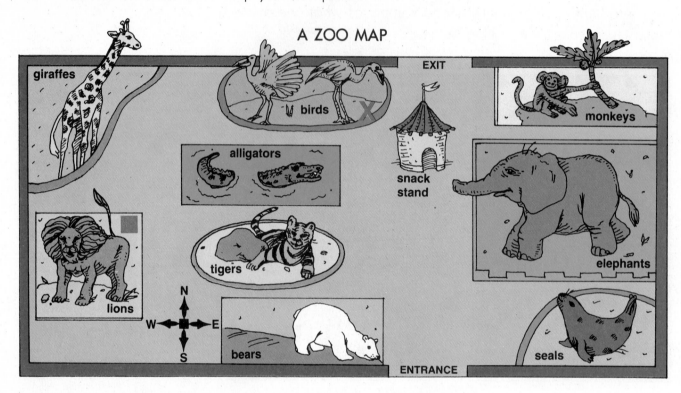

A ZOO MAP

Pretend you and your family are planning a trip to the zoo.
Use the map and labels to help you see where the animals are.

1. Which animals are on your left as you
   enter the zoo? _____

2. Which animals are farther from the seals —
   the alligators or the giraffes? _____

3. Which animals are in the largest area? _____

4. Which two animals would you see as you
   leave the zoo? _____

5. On the map, draw a path from the **entrance** to the **exit**.
   Go **between** the following: bears and tigers, lions and tigers,
   alligators and giraffes, birds and alligators, snack stand and
   elephants, and monkeys and snack stand.

MAIN DIRECTIONS

North, south, east, and **west.** Do you remember these words?
They are the four **main directions**. A compass rose like the one
below shows directions on a map.

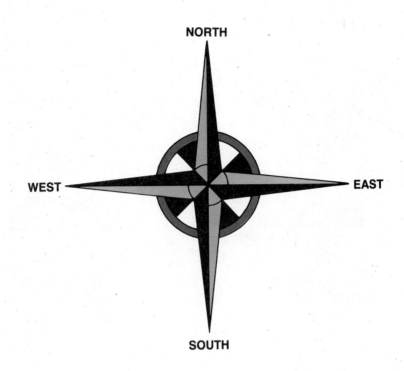

Look at the map on page 6. Can you find the compass rose?
Circle it. Then use it to find your way around the zoo, and
answer the questions below.

1. To get from the entrance to the elephants, which
   direction should you walk?

   _____

2. A zoo keeper fed the birds at **X**. She is going
   to feed the bears. She will take the shortest path.
   Which direction will she walk?

   _____

3. You have bought ice cream at the snack stand.
   You go to meet your parents at the giraffe area.
   Which direction do you walk?

   _____

4. You have seen all the animals. You and your family
   want to leave the zoo. You are at the ▪ near the lions.   _____
   Find the shortest path to the exit. In which direction do
   you go first? Then which direction do you go?

   _____

Using directions . . . on your own

People in Grovetown reported that there were holes in their
streets. So the Grovetown Street Department is sending truck
drivers out to find the holes. The drivers are using this map. The
holes are **numbered.** Study the map and the compass rose.
Answer the questions below.

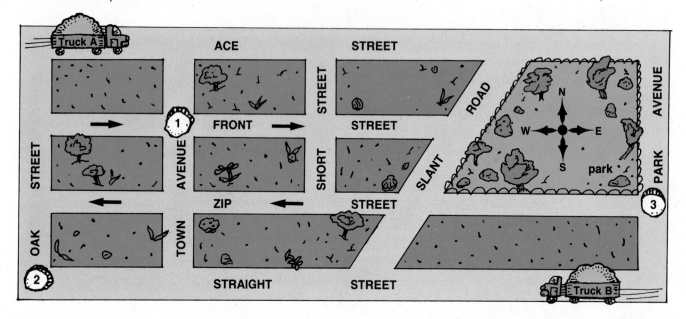

1. In what direction should **Truck A** go to reach Town Ave.? _____

2. In what direction should **Truck A** go on Town Ave. to
   reach **Hole 1**? _____

3. In what direction should **Truck B** go to find **Hole 2**? _____

4. Zip St. and Front St. are **one way** streets. The arrows
   show in what direction people may drive. In what
   direction can the trucks drive?

   on Zip St.: _____   **on Front St.:** _____

5. On the map, use a colored pencil to draw the shortest route
   for **Truck B** to get from **Hole 2** to **Hole 3.**

6. Is there another route **Truck B** can take to reach **Hole 3**?
   Draw it on the map. Use a different color for your line.

Finding main directions . . . on your own

You can find the directions on a map by looking at a compass rose. And you can find directions on land with a compass. A compass has a special magnet that always points **north.**

But suppose you do not have a compass. Here's a way to figure out directions:

Stand outdoors at noon. Your shadow will always point north. When you know where north is, you can find the other directions.

Pretend you are the child in the drawing. Use your shadow to figure out different directions.

1. Your shadow points north. You are facing north. Where is south?

   in front of you   behind you   to your right

2. You are still facing north. Where is west?

   to your right   to your left   behind you

3. Now you turn and face west. Your shadow is still pointing north. Where is east?

   to your right   to your left   behind you

4. If you turn and face south, where is west?

   to your left   to your right   behind you

5. If you turn and face north, where is east?

   to your right   behind you   in front of you

6. If you turn and face east, where is north?

   behind you   to your right   to your left

IN-BETWEEN DIRECTIONS

Sometimes a place is between the main directions.
Then we use **in-between direction** words. They are:

northeast   southeast   southwest   northwest

The compass rose below shows **north, south, east,** and **west.**
The in-between direction **northeast** is shown **halfway** between
north and east. **Southeast** is **halfway** between east and south.

On the compass rose, write the missing **in-between directions.**
You may use the word or the abbreviation. **Northeast** is written
for you.

northeast	NE	southwest	SW
southeast	SE	northwest	NW

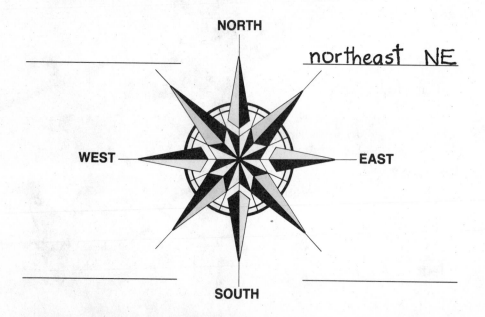

northeast NE

The arrow at the right is pointing **north.**

1. Add a line going from **southwest** to **northeast.**
   Go through the dot.
   At the **northeast** end, put an arrow point.

2. Now add a line going from **northwest** to **southeast.**
   Go through the dot.
   At the **southeast** end, put an arrow point.

Practice with in-between directions

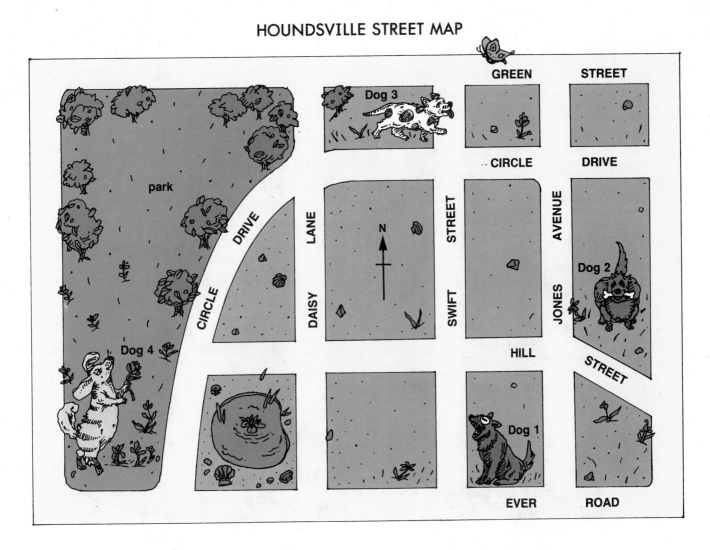

HOUNDSVILLE STREET MAP

Mr. Barkley is the dog catcher in Houndsville.
He is rounding up the stray dogs in town.
This map shows where four of them are.
Help Mr. Barkley find them.
Label each sentence true (**T**) or false (**F**).

_____ **1.** Dog 1 is near the corner of
Swift Street and Ever Road.

_____ **2.** Dog 2 is west of dog 1.

_____ **3.** Dog 2 is southeast of dog 3.

_____ **4.** Dog 4 is in the northern end
of the park.

_____ **5.** Dog 3 is north of Circle Drive.

_____ **6.** Dog 4 is southwest of dog 3.

Using in-between directions . . . on your own

Sometimes, a map does not have a compass rose to show directions. You will see only an **arrow** pointing **north**.

Look at the **north arrow** on this map. Circle the letter that stands for **north**. Then on the north arrow, write **E** for **east**, **S** for **south**, and **W** for **west**.

MAIN STREET TOY SHOP

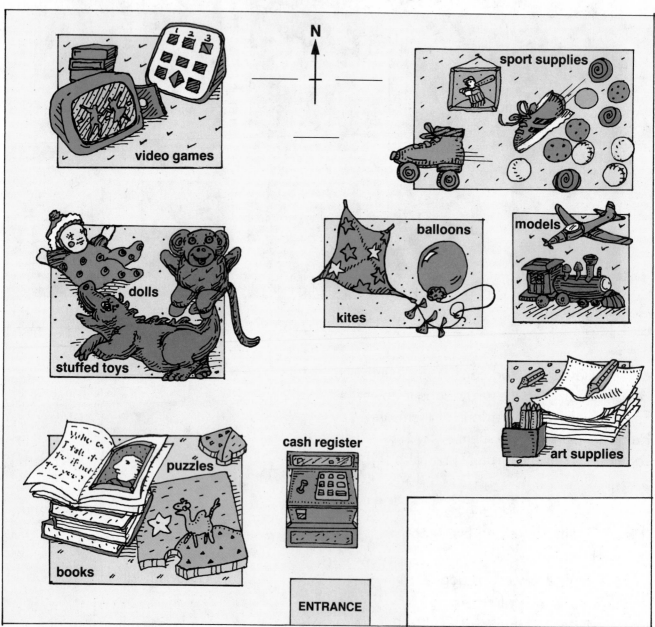

Can you find your way around the toy store? Use the map on page 12 to answer each question with an **in-between direction**.

1. In which part of the store can you find skates? _____

2. Your friend has been looking at video games.
   You are going to meet at the art counter.
   In what direction should your friend walk
   to get to the art counter? _____

3. You have just picked out a model airplane.
   You go to the cash register to pay for it.
   In what direction do you walk? _____

4. Add toys and a sign to the empty counter on the map.
   Which direction is the counter from:

   a. the balloons? _____

   b. the puzzles? _____

   c. the dolls and stuffed toys? _____

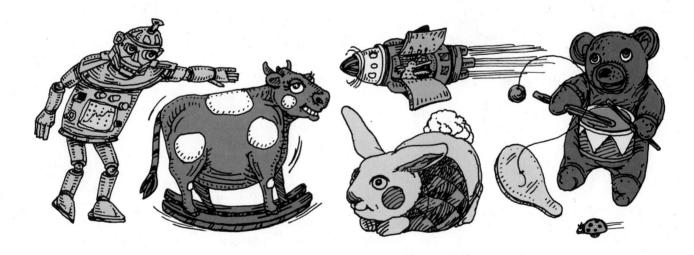

5. Suppose you and a friend want to buy the following items: a
   video tape, a book, a kite, a pair of running shoes, and a
   box of paints. On the map, check (✔) each counter you will
   go to. Then use a colored pencil to draw the shortest path
   from one counter to the other. Start at the Entrance. Finish at
   the cash register.

REVIEW

Now show how much you have learned about maps. Read each sentence. Put a check (✔) next to each one that is true.

_____ 1. A map is a drawing of all or part of our planet.

_____ 2. The four main directions are north, south, east, and southwest.

_____ 3. There are no in-between directions.

_____ 4. A globe is a model of our round planet.

_____ 5. A compass rose shows directions on a map.

_____ 6. If you know only one direction, you cannot figure out any other direction.

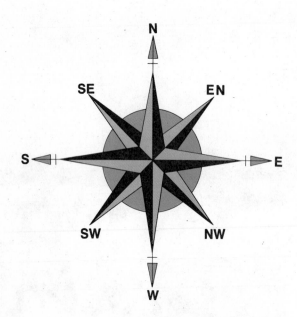

7. Oops! The mapmaker slipped up here. Five directions on this compass rose are mixed up. Can you correct them? Cross out the wrong directions. Write in the correct ones.

8. Look at the abbreviations for directions below. On the lines, write the words they stand for.

N _____   NW _____

E _____   SE _____

Finley City has set aside an area of land near a park. People in the city can use this land to plant vegetable gardens. This map shows part of the garden area. A sign shows who uses each garden. You can also see what is planted in each garden. Use the map to do the work below.

VEGETABLE GARDENS IN FINLEY CITY

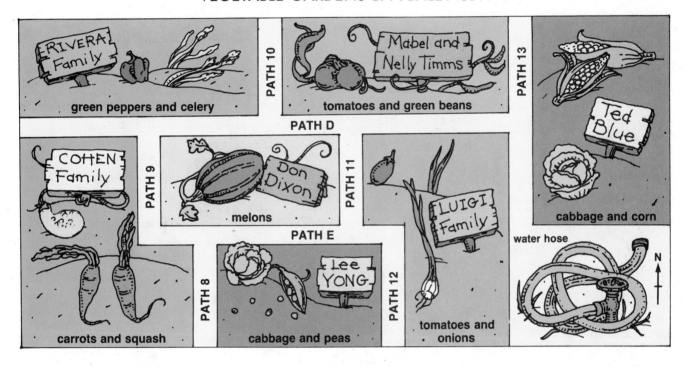

Read each sentence. On the line, write **T** for a true sentence. Write **F** for a false one.

_____ 1. The Cohens use the garden in the southwest corner.

_____ 2. Cabbage and corn grow in the northwest garden.

_____ 3. The Rivera family's garden is near Path 10 and Path D.

_____ 4. Ted Blue's garden is farther north than Lee Yong's.

_____ 5. The garden to the west of Don Dixon's plot has peas.

_____ 6. The hose for watering the plants is east of most plots.

7. Draw a path to show the shortest distance from Lee Yong's garden to the hose.

Imagine you are an astronaut visiting a strange planet. You see many unusual places and give them names. You make a map to show people on Earth where you have been. You **number** the places you see in the **order** in which you come to them. But you forget to label them on your map.

Look at the list of places below. In the boxes on the map, **label** each place in the **order** in which you saw it.

1. Spaghetti Field   **4.** Red Rocks
2. Square Forest   **5.** Bumpy Mountains
3. Swirly Lake   **6.** Spooky Valley

Now follow the numbers on the map. Draw your route.
Write a title for your map.

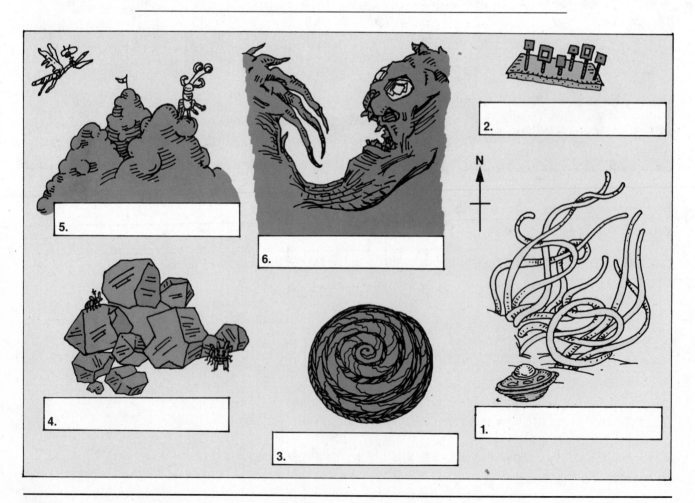

Computer fun

A **flowchart** is a drawing of **steps** for a computer.
Each step is listed in the **order** it must be done.

After you explore this strange planet, you start to make the
flowchart below. It will help other astronauts when they explore
your new planet.

Some of the information has been filled in. Look at the map on
page 16. Use it to finish filling in the flowchart.

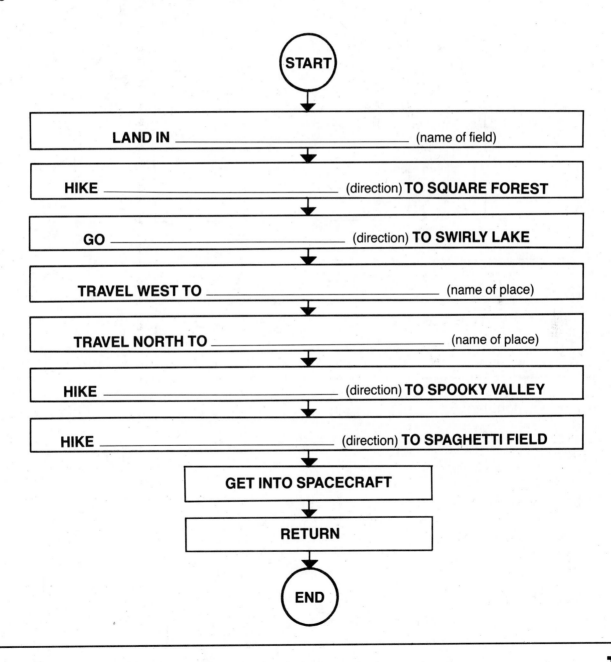

START

LAND IN _____ (name of field)

HIKE _____ (direction) **TO SQUARE FOREST**

GO _____ (direction) **TO SWIRLY LAKE**

TRAVEL WEST TO _____ (name of place)

TRAVEL NORTH TO _____ (name of place)

HIKE _____ (direction) **TO SPOOKY VALLEY**

HIKE _____ (direction) **TO SPAGHETTI FIELD**

GET INTO SPACECRAFT

RETURN

END

SYMBOLS

Imagine you are floating near the ceiling of a house. You look down and see the rooms below you. That's what the map below shows.

In this map, the **lines** stand for **walls.** The **blank spaces** stand for **doors.** The map tells you something more. But the information is in a kind of code. In the code, the ▲ (triangle) and the **X** stand for children playing a game of hide-and-seek. The ▲ is a child who is hiding. The **X** is the child who is IT—looking for the others.

Look at the map and answer the questions below.

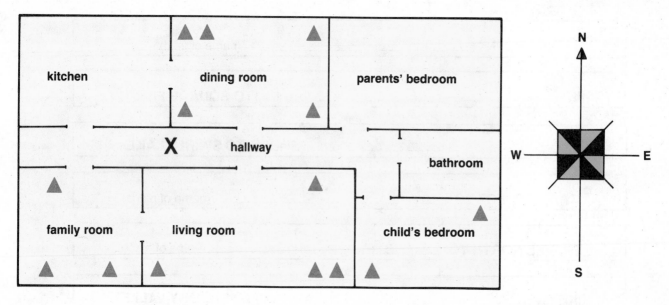

1. Where is IT standing? _____

2. How many children are hiding? _____

3. In which room is the child nearest IT hiding? _____

4. In which room are only two children hiding? _____

5. How many children are hiding in the room east of the kitchen? _____

On the map, the ▲ and the **X** are **symbols.**
Symbols are drawings that **stand for real things.**

Practice with symbols

Some map symbols stand for **natural areas** such as **lakes, rivers, hills,** or **mountains.** Other symbols show things **people have built,** such as **buildings, bridges, railroads,** or **airports.** Symbols often look something like the real objects or places they stand for. Below are photographs of six things often shown on maps. Next to the photographs are symbols that can be used for those items on a map.

1. Circle the symbols that stand for **natural areas.**

2. Underline the symbols that stand for things **people have built.**

3. At the right is a **key** for the **symbols** above.
   It tells what the symbols stand for.
   It is only partly filled in. Some symbols and labels are missing. Fill in the missing parts in the key.

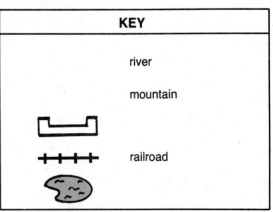

KEY
river
mountain
railroad

More practice with symbols

Mapmakers use many different symbols to show information on a map. The **map key** or **legend** shows what the symbols stand for.

Look at the map and its title. What does the map show you?

_____

The map was made for a girl named Emily. She and her family have just moved to Springville. The map will help her find her school and other places in her new neighborhood.

EMILY'S NEIGHBORHOOD IN SPRINGVILLE

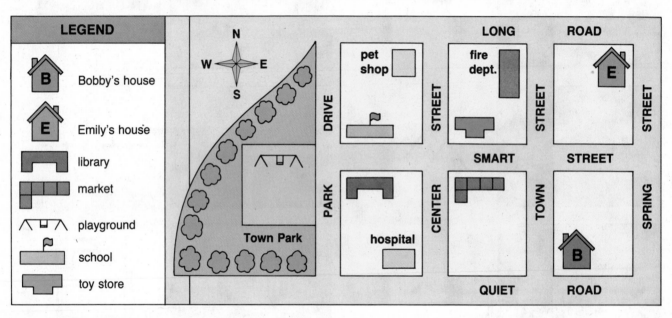

1. Look at the Legend. What does ⌐▭ stand for? _____

2. What building is just south of the school? _____

3. At the corner of which two streets does Emily live?

   _____   _____

4. How many blocks is Emily's house from school? _____

5. What direction is the playground from Emily's house? _____

6. Emily and Bobby walk from their own houses to
   the toy store. Who has the shorter walk? _____

20

From a photograph to a map

The photograph at the right was taken from an airplane, high above the roads and buildings. The map shows the **same area** as the photograph. Some things in the photograph are shown as **symbols** on the map. But the map does **not** show everything you see in the photograph.

1. Name one thing you see in the photograph and not on the map.

   _____

2. Name two things on the map that are not in the photograph.

   _____

   _____

3. Name two things that are in the map and the photograph. Circle them on the map and in the photograph.

   _____

   _____

4. Which shows you there are a lot of cars in this area — the map or the photograph?

   _____

5. Which tells you the direction in which you are driving— the map or the photograph?

   _____

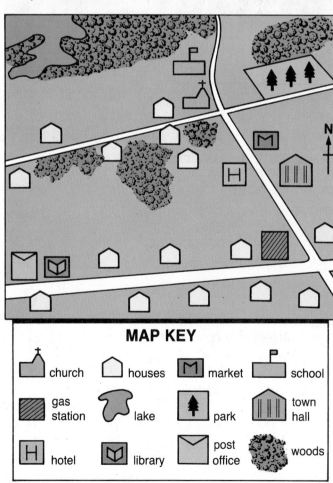

MAP KEY

church houses M market school

gas station lake park town hall

H hotel library post office woods

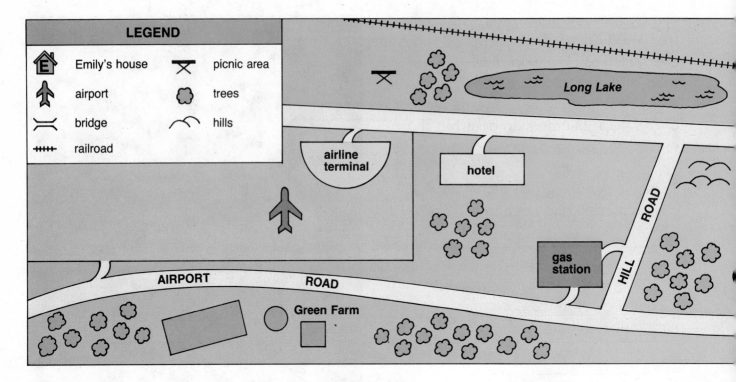

On page 20, you saw a map of Emily's neighborhood in Springville. The map on pages 22 and 23 shows more of Springville. Emily lives in the **eastern** part of the town. Her house is on the corner of **Long Road** and **Spring Street**. Circle her house on the map.

Emily's cousin and grandparents are coming to visit. Use the map to answer these questions.

1. Emily and her family walk to the railroad station to meet Emily's cousin. About how many blocks is their house from the station? _____

2. They drive from the station to the airport. They go along the road just south of the railroad tracks. What is the name of this road? _____

3. How many bridges do they cross? _____

4. What natural area south of the road do they pass? _____

5. What is the building on Long Road just east of the airport? _____

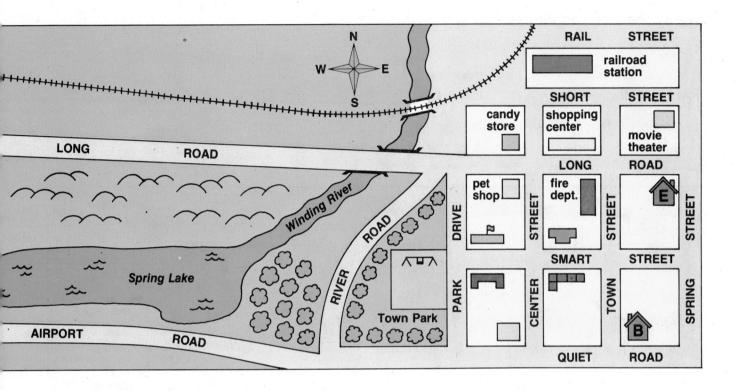

People often look for **landmarks** when they are walking or driving. Landmarks can be lakes, parks, buildings, statues, or other things. Landmarks help people know if they are on the right road. Emily and her family see a hotel just before they get to the airport. That is the landmark they are looking for.

On the way home from the airport, the family drives along Hill Road and Airport Road.

1. What is one landmark to look for just north of Airport Road? _____

2. In what direction does the family drive on Airport Road? _____

3. They want to turn onto Park Drive. What landmark will they look for just before Park Drive? _____

4. On Hill Road, Emily had seen a picnic area. That landmark is not on the map. Look at the Legend. Then on the map, north of Spring Lake, draw the symbol for a picnic area.

Symbols for towns and cities

The **symbols** below are used on most maps to show **cities, towns,** and **capital cities.**

○ •
town, small city

◉ •
large city

✪ ★
capital city

The map on this page shows places in the United States where Emily's relatives live. Study the map and answer the questions below.

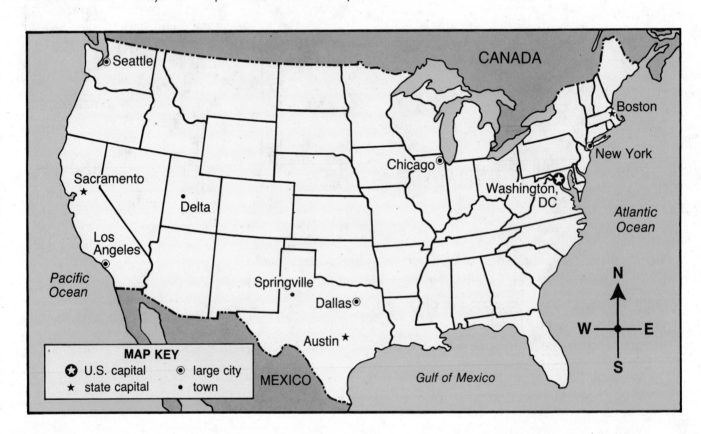

1. Emily comes from a small town in Texas.
   Underline the name of her town on the map.

2. Emily's grandparents live in a large city
   in the far northwest. What is its name? _____

3. Emily's uncle lives in the capital of
   the United States. Circle the city on
   the map. Write its name on the line. _____

4. Emily's cousin lives in the capital of a
   state in the northeast. What is its name? _____

Using symbols . . . on your own

Emily's grandparents visited her at school in Springville, Texas. They saw her class do a special project. Each child sent a balloon into the air. Each balloon had a note tied to it. The note asked the finder of the balloon to write back and tell where the balloon had landed. This map shows the places where 10 balloons were found. Use it to answer the questions below.

1. Find the balloon that flew farthest north. In which city did it land?

_____

2. Two balloons landed in capital cities. What cities were they?

_____

_____

3. One balloon landed in a city northwest of Emily's state. Name that city.

_____

4. Three balloons landed in Emily's state. Two of them landed in towns. Name them.

_____

_____

Using colors and patterns

Colors can be symbols. For example, **water** is usually **blue.** Park or **forest** areas are often **green.** On the map below, color all the water areas blue. Color all park and forest areas green. Answer the questions below the map.

LAKE VILLAGE

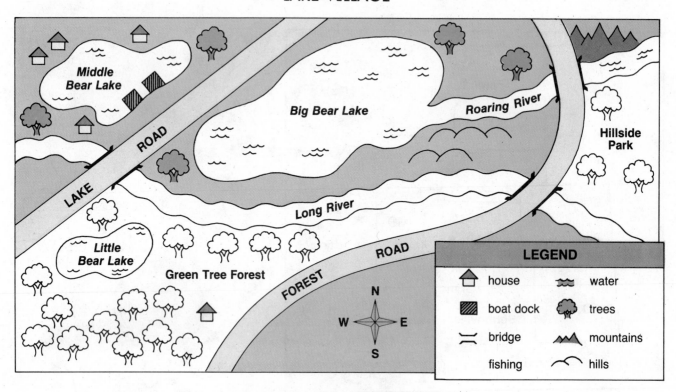

1. Look at the map title. What does the map tell you about? _____

2. How many lakes are in Lake Village? _____

3. Which lake has houses near it? _____

4. Which lake is in a forest? _____

5. How many bridges go over Long River? _____

6. To get from Little Bear Lake to Big Bear Lake, in which direction would you go? _____

7. In the Legend, draw a **symbol** for **fishing.** On the map, put your symbol where fishing can take place.

More work with colors and patterns

Patterns such as stripes or diamonds can also be symbols. The map below uses different patterns and colors to tell about thunderstorms in 48 of the U.S. states. Read each question below the map. Then look carefully at the Map Key and the map. Underline the best answer to each question.

NUMBER OF DAYS WITH THUNDERSTORMS

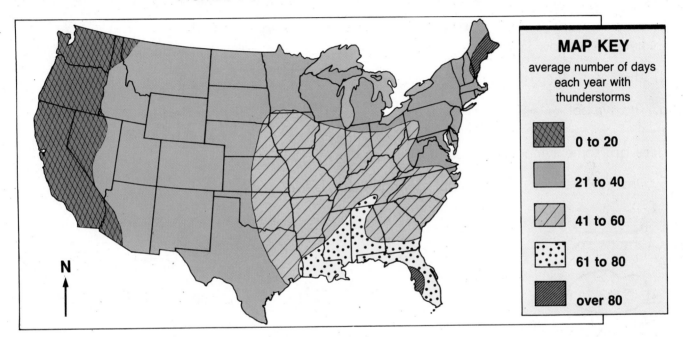

1. What pattern is used to show areas that have 41 to 60 days with thunderstorms each year?

   dots   diamonds   stripes

2. How many days with thunderstorms are there each year in the dotted area?

   0 to 20   61 to 80   21 to 40

3. In which part of the United States shown on this map do the fewest thunderstorms take place?

   the north   the west   the east

4. Two small areas in the United States have more than 80 days a year with thunderstorms. In what parts of the country are these areas?

   northeast and southeast   center and north   west and south

REVIEW

The word or words that fit in each blank below are at the end of each sentence. But the letters are all mixed up. Read the sentences and write the correct words in the blanks.

1. A _____ tells what the symbols on a map stand for.   amp yke

2. The opposite of northeast is _____.   hosutstew

3. A _____ such as a statue or a building helps you know if you are on the right road.   ladnmkar

4. The color blue on a map often means _____.   arewt

5. The symbol ┼┼┼ stands for _____.   laridaro

Here are some symbols often used on maps.

6. Draw a line from each symbol to what it stands for.

river

mountains

bridge

lake

hills

You have learned a great deal about maps, directions, and symbols. Show how much you know. Look at the map on page 29. Underline the words that will finish each sentence below correctly.

7. Five states in the west with mountains are _____.

Nevada   Colorado   New York   Oregon   Iowa   Utah   Arizona

8. Four states that have no mountains are _____.

Georgia   Kansas   North Dakota   Oklahoma   Alabama   Ohio

UNITED STATES

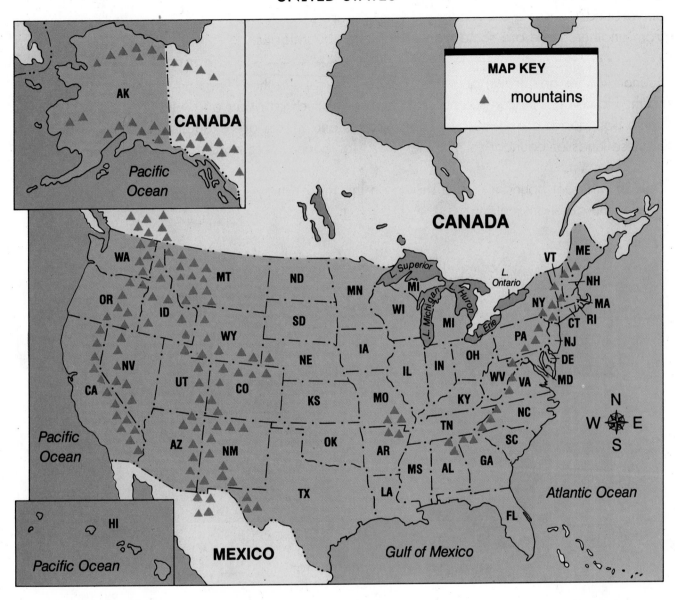

Look at the map to find the answers to these riddles.

1. I'm a state in the far west. I'm long and thin. I have mountains. The ocean is west of me. What's my name? _____

2. I'm a state in the south. I'm so big that about nine northeast states could fit inside me. What's my name? _____

3. I'm a state in the north. I'm divided into two parts by a large lake. What's my name? _____

BOUNDARIES AND BORDERS

Do you have a fence or wall near your home, school, or playground? Fences are **boundaries.** They **separate** one area from another. Here are some map symbols for boundaries:

• • • • • • • • • • • • ———————— – – – – – – ○○○○○○○○○○○○

Boundary lines are drawn on maps, but you do not see these lines on Earth. However, you can see **natural** boundaries such as **rivers** and **lakes.** Some boundaries are **made** by people. **Roads** and **fences** are examples of these kinds of boundaries. Another word for **boundary** is **border.**

Several different boundaries are shown on this map. Study it to answer the questions below.

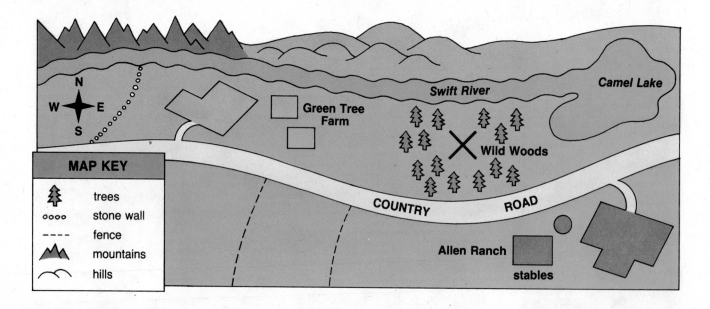

1. How many different boundaries are around the farm? _____

2. What is the boundary on Green Tree Farm to the

   north? _____   south? _____

   east? _____   west? _____

3. The X on the map shows where foxes have been seen. A fence will be put up to keep the foxes away from the farm. On the map, draw a fence in the best place to keep the foxes away. (Look at the Map Key for the symbol.)

Practice with boundaries and borders

Some of our western states and part of Canada are on the map below.
The **boundaries**, or **borders**, between the **states** are shown this way: — . — . —
The **borders** between the **United States** and **Canada** are shown this way: — .. — .. —
Use the map to answer the questions below.

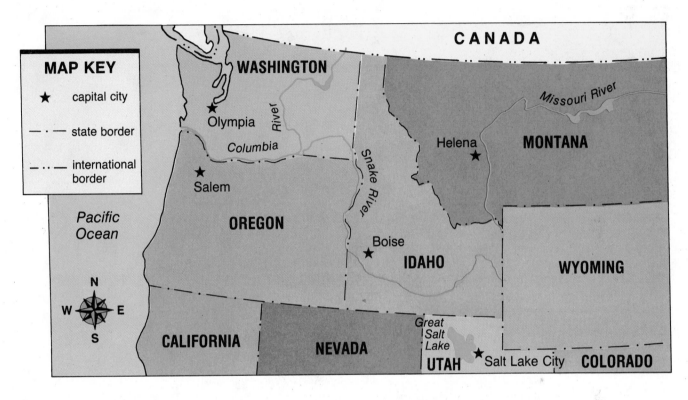

1. What symbol is used to show boundaries between the states? Draw the symbol in the space below.

2. What symbol is used to show the boundary between the two countries? Draw the symbol in the space below.

3. Name three states that border Idaho.

_____ _____ _____

4. What river forms part of the border between the states of Washington and Oregon? _____

5. Suppose you want to travel to Canada. From which states shown on this map could you enter Canada?

_____

Borders of the United States and North America

This map shows the continent of North America. You can see the United States and the two countries that **border** it. Use the map to answer the questions below.

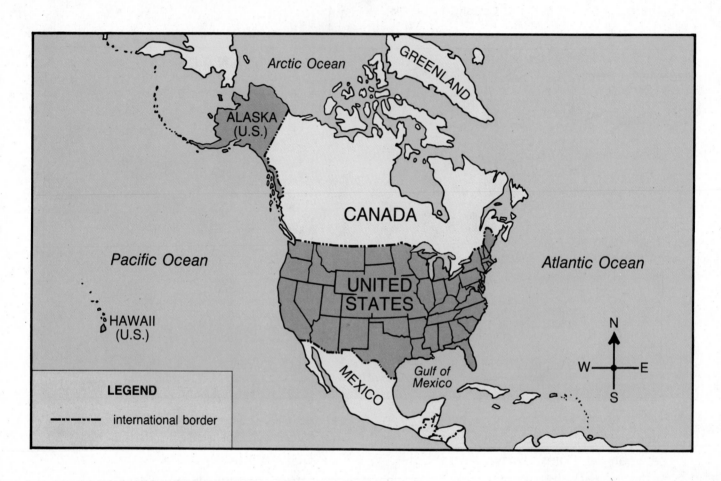

1. Which country borders the United States to the north? _____

2. Which country borders the United States to the south? _____

3. What symbol is used to show the borders between the United States and its neighbors? _____

4. Which ocean borders North America on the east? _____

5. Which ocean borders North America on the west? _____

6. Which U.S. state is in the most northwestern part of the continent of North America? _____

7. Which U.S. state is not part of North America? _____

Continents, oceans, and their borders

North America is one of seven **continents** in the world. Continents are the largest bodies of land on our planet. This world map shows the continents and the oceans that border them.

THE WORLD

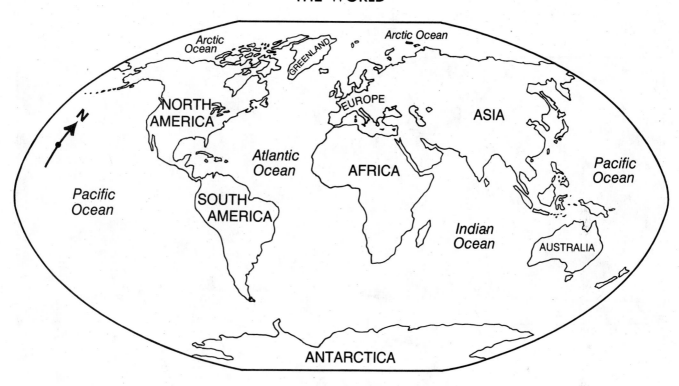

1. On the map, circle the names of each of the seven continents.

2. Which continent is farthest south? _____

3. Name the four oceans of the world.

   _____   _____

   _____   _____

4. Which ocean is the only one that does not border North America? _____

5. On the map, color the water blue. Color each continent a different color.

BODIES OF LAND AND WATER

Continents are the largest bodies of land on Earth. Oceans are the largest bodies of water. There are also special names for smaller land and water shapes or areas on Earth.

The picture shows some land and water areas you see on many maps. You can read about each one of them below the picture.

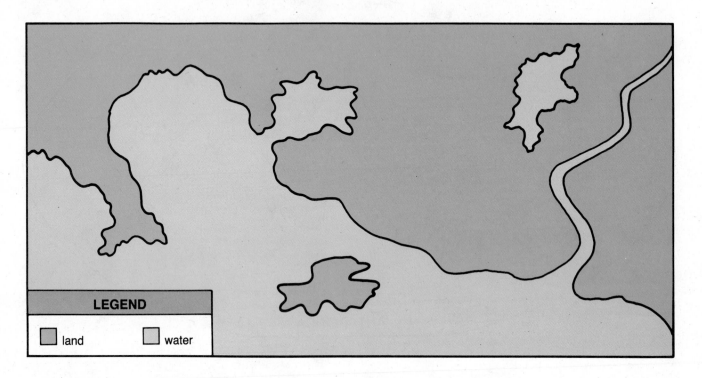

LEGEND
☐ land   ☐ water

Read each meaning. Write the letter for each one on the correct land or water area in the picture.

A. sea—another word for ocean. A large lake of salt water or fresh water can also be a sea.

B. bay—a small part of an ocean, sea, or lake that cuts into the land.

C. gulf—like a bay, but larger.

D. lake—a large body of water with land all around it.

E. river—a large stream of water that flows into a larger river or other body of water.

F. coast, shore—the edge of land, where it meets a body of water.

G. island—land with water all around it.

H. peninsula—land that sticks far out into a body of water. It has water on three sides of it.

Practice naming the shapes

Alaska has many different kinds of land and water shapes. Some of them are numbered on this map. Look at each number. What is the word for the area on which the number appears? Write the number next to the correct word below the map.

ALASKA

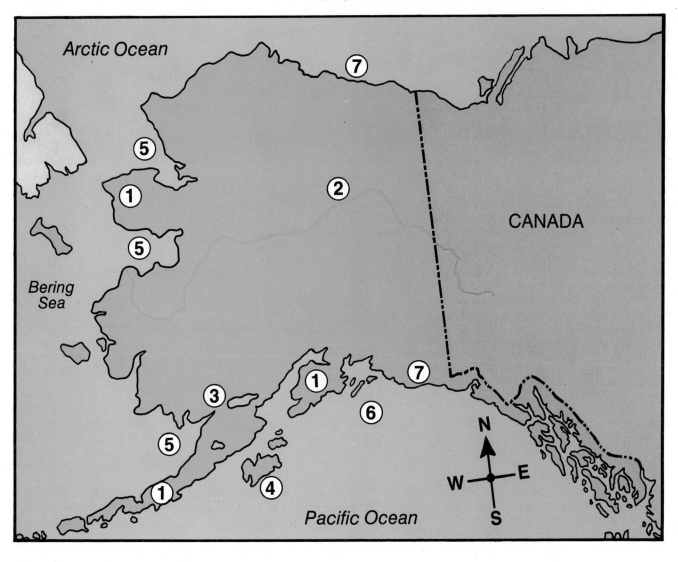

river _____   gulf _____   peninsula _____   lake _____

coast _____   bay _____   island _____

What is the symbol for the border between the
United States and Canada? Draw it at the right.

HIGHLANDS AND LOWLANDS

Some places on Earth are several thousand feet high. Other places are flat and much lower. Earth has lands of different heights and shapes. The picture shows you some of them. Read about them below the picture.

A. **hills**–land that is higher than the land around it.

B. **mountains**–very high hills, sometimes very steep. A long row of mountains is called a mountain range.

C. **peak**–the top of a mountain.

D. **valley**–low land between hills or mountains.

E. **plain**–a wide area of flat land, often not very high.

F. **plateau**–high land that is usually rather flat.

1. Look at the picture. What place does each definition tell about? Write the letter for each definition on that kind of land in the picture.

2. Maps are flat. But they can use symbols to show high and low land. You already know two symbols for high lands. Draw the symbols next to the words below.

mountains   **hills**

3. Now make up and draw a symbol for each kind of land below.

valley   **plateau**

Practice seeing highlands and lowlands

Mapmakers can show highlands and lowlands in another way—
with **color**. A map key might show lowlands and hills in **green**.
High mountains might be **brown**. In-between lands, such as
plateaus, might be **yellow** or **orange**.

The colors on this map show several
kinds of land. Use the Map Key to
learn what the colors stand for.

1. How many kinds of land
   are shown on the map?

   _____

2. Which color stands for
   the highest land?

   _____

3. Which color stands for
   the lowest land?

   _____

4. Which color stands for
   plateau areas?

   _____

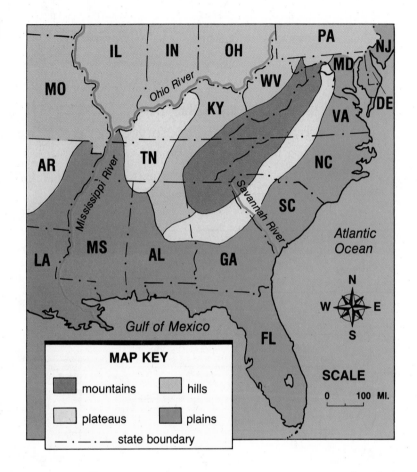

Underline the words below that finish each sentence correctly.

5. A state with high mountains is _____.   Mississippi   Virginia

6. The plains in North Carolina are _____.   near the shore   in the west

7. A state with a large area of hills is _____.   Florida   West Virginia

8. You could go mountain climbing in _____.   North Carolina   Alabama

9. Suppose you are a farmer in Georgia.
   You will find more flat land for
   farming in _____.   the north   the south

REVIEW

What do you know?

1. Look at the groups of words below. Cross out the one word
   in each row that does not belong.

   A. lake   river   island   ocean
   B. continent   island   peninsula   lake
   C. mountain   bay   hill   plateau

2. Look at the map at the right. What
   is shown by each letter? Choose your
   answer from the word box below.
   Write your answer on the line next
   to the correct letter.

valley	river	lake
island	coast	peak

   A. _____

   B. _____

   C. _____

   D. _____

   E. _____

   F. _____

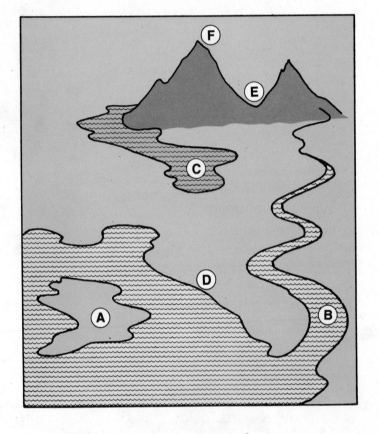

3. Look at the map on the next page. Then underline the words
   that best complete these sentences.

   A. Florida is _____.

      a continent   an island   a peninsula

   B. There are _____ along the boundary between the United States
      and Canada.

      five big lakes   two small oceans   a group of islands

This map shows the Mississippi River and two of its branches. The branches flow into the Mississippi River. Use the map to answer the questions below it.

THREE LONG RIVERS OF THE UNITED STATES

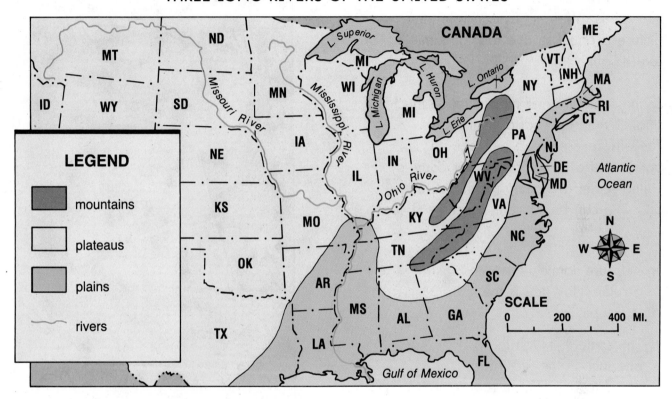

1. Name the two rivers on the map that are branches of the Mississippi River.

   _____   _____

2. Name three states that border the Ohio River.

   _____   _____   _____

3. Name two states that have the Missouri River as part of their border.

   _____   _____

4. Imagine you are taking a boat trip all the way down the
   Mississippi River. You start in the far north, where the river
   begins. How many states that border the river will you pass?   _____

MEASURING DISTANCE

Jamie had his picture drawn at his school fair. He was dressed as a magician. Jamie is really four feet tall. But in the picture he is only four inches tall. The picture looks like Jamie, only the size is different. **One inch** in the picture is equal to **one foot** of Jamie's real height.

In the same way, a map is made much smaller than the real area it shows. The difference in size between an object and a larger or smaller copy is called **scale.** The **scale** for the picture of Jamie can be written: **1 inch = 1 foot**

1. Measure Jamie's hat with a ruler. How tall is the hat in the picture? _____

2. The **scale** tells you that **one inch** in the picture is equal to **one foot** in real life. What is the real height of Jamie's hat? _____

3. In the picture, measure the wand that Jamie holds. How long is it? _____

4. How long would the real wand be? _____

5. Jamie's parents had a very small copy of the picture made. They wanted it to fit into a tiny frame. What is the scale of the new picture at the right? _____

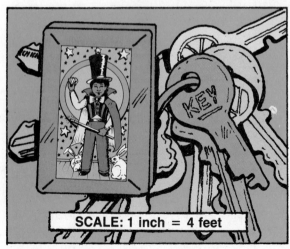

SCALE: 1 inch = 4 feet

Practice with a map scale

Boontown and Happy Hills are villages in Darwin County. Use this map of Darwin County to find out how far people travel there. Look at the bottom of the map. What is the **scale** you will use? _____

To answer the questions below, measure the distance between places on the map. Use the scale to find the real distances.

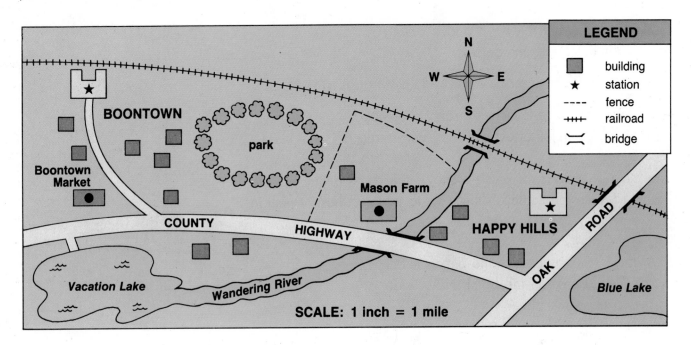

1. Pablo lives in Boontown. He goes to Happy Hills on the train. The two stations are marked on the map with this symbol: ★
   a. What is the distance in a straight line on the map between the two stations? _____
   b. Now use the map scale. How many miles is it really between the two stations? _____

2. Ms. Mason takes eggs from her farm to the market in Boontown. The farm and the market are marked with this symbol: ● Measure the distance between the symbols and use the map scale. How many miles does Ms. Mason travel to market? _____

3. Imagine you are on vacation and visit Vacation Lake. You drive south from Happy Hills Station on Oak Road. Then you drive on County Highway to Vacation Lake. About how many miles in all is your trip? _____

More practice with map scales

Some map scales look like a kind of ruler. Look at scale A.

On scale A, ½ inch = ½ mile.

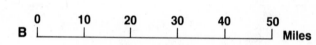

1. How many miles does 1 inch equal? _____

2. How many miles do 2½ inches equal? _____

Now look at scale B. Use it and a ruler to answer the questions below.

3. On scale B, how many miles is 1 inch equal to? _____

4. If two cities are 2 inches apart on a map, how many miles apart are they with scale B? _____

The map on pages 42 and 43 shows the route of the Long Line Railroad. Use the scale on the map to answer these questions.

5. What is ½ inch equal to on the scale? _____

6. With a ruler, measure the distance across the lake (between the dots). How wide is the lake on the map? _____

7. What is the real distance across the lake? _____

Now you are ready to learn more about places and distances on this map by answering the questions on page 43.

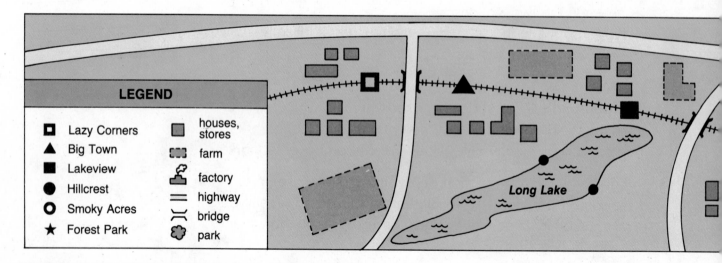

Using the scale . . . on your own

The railroad station for each town on the map is marked by a special symbol. Read the Legend to learn the name of each town. Use the scale to figure out the distances. Then answer each question below.

1. Daisy and her brother Dennis live in Lazy Corners. They go to Big Town to get new shoes. What is the distance on the map between the two stations? _____

2. How far is the real trip? _____

3. Ms. Morgan is on her way from Lakeview to Hillcrest to see a movie. How far does she travel on the train? _____

4. Mr. Jenner ordered garden seeds from a store in Smoky Acres. He lives in Forest Park. The package was sent by Railroad Express. How far did the package travel? _____

5. Susy and her family live in Smoky Acres. The family is going by train to a fair in Hillcrest. How many miles will they travel? _____

6. Benji's parents have a farm in Lazy Corners. Put a check on the farm. Benji's family is going to the fair by train. How much farther is Benji's train trip than Susy's? _____

7. A new factory is built in Big Town. On the map, draw the symbol for a factory. Put it south of the houses and stores in Big Town.

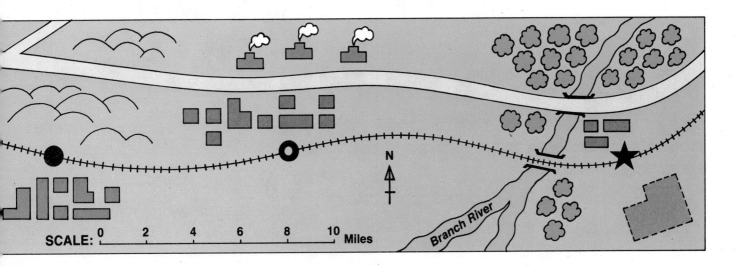

SCALE: 0 2 4 6 8 10 Miles

Branch River

Two ways of measuring

Here is the kind of ruler many children have in their classrooms.
One side of the ruler shows inches. The other side shows centimeters.

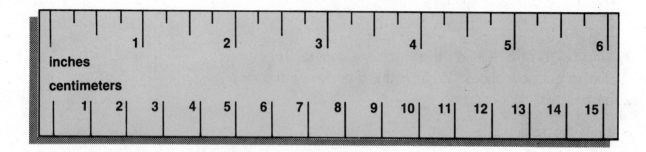

There are two systems for measuring in use today. Many people measure in **inches** (in.), **feet** (ft.), **yards** (yd.), and **miles** (mi.). Many others use the **metric system.** They measure in **centimeters** (cm), **meters** (m), and **kilometers** (km). The units in each system are different lengths. For example, inches are longer than centimeters. Miles are longer than kilometers.

Copy the centimeter ruler above. Find out how long places are on Wiggle Island. Measure between the dots.

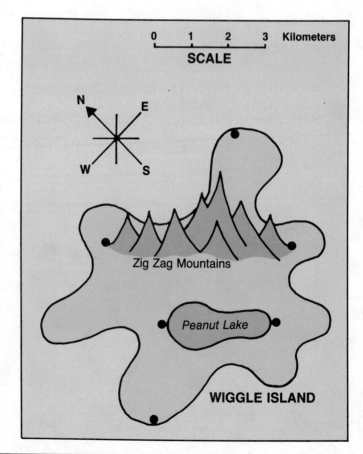

1. How many **centimeters** wide is Peanut Lake? _____

2. How many **kilometers** wide is Peanut Lake? _____

3. If you wanted to hike from one end of Zig Zag Mountains to the other, how many **kilometers** would you walk? _____

4. How many **kilometers** long is Wiggle Island at its longest point? _____

Using scales . . . on your own

Here's an easy way to use a scale on a map. It works for a scale of miles and a scale of kilometers.

Put the edge of a piece of paper along the two points you want to measure. On the edge of the paper mark where these points are. Then hold the marked edge of the paper along the map scale to figure out the real distance.

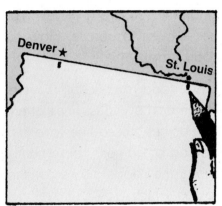

Use both scales on this map to find the distances between some big cities in the U.S. and to answer the questions below.

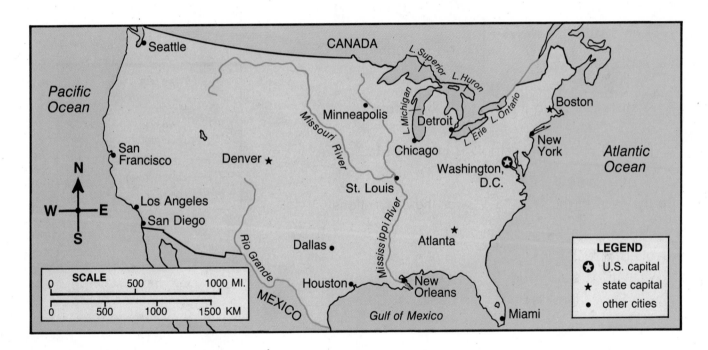

1. Dan Darby flew with his parents from Seattle to San Diego. About how far did they travel from Seattle to San Diego?

   in miles: _____   in kilometers: _____

2. Mrs. Haney lives in Chicago. She flies to Boston for business. On her way home, she stops in Washington, D.C. and then flies home.

   a. About how far is her trip to Boston?   in miles: _____   in kilometers: _____

   b. About how far in all is her return trip?   in miles: _____   in kilometers: _____

UNDERSTANDING ROAD MAPS

Imagine you are a driver. You need to go to a town you have never been to before. How can you find your way? You use a road map!

On a road map, certain symbols give people information for driving. The widest lines often stand for the widest highways. Sometimes, these lines are red. Most main roads have **numbers** instead of names. These numbers are shown on road maps. Signs along the roads also show these numbers. Drivers look for them to see which way to travel.

Here are some road symbols used on road maps:

interstate highways ⎫
U.S. highways   ⎬ go through **many states.**

state roads go through only **one state.**

small roads connect towns in **one state.**

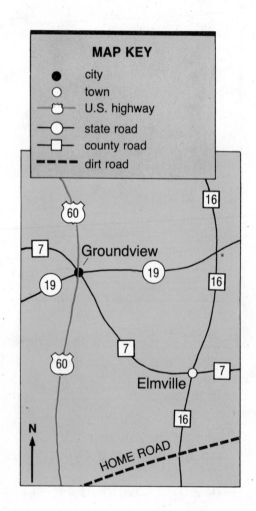

Use the map at the right to answer these questions.

1. A road is sometimes called a route. Is Route 19 a state road or a U.S. highway? _____

2. Is Route 7 a state road or a smaller one? _____

3. Which road is a dirt road? _____

4. Which routes go through Groundview? _____

5. Which one road will take you from Groundview to Elmville? _____

Using a road map

Ms. Ford is a salesperson. She hopes to sell blue jeans to a store in Oakhurst. She has never been there, so she is using this road map to find her way. Ms. Ford lives in Dixon.

CENTER CITY AND NEIGHBORING TOWNS

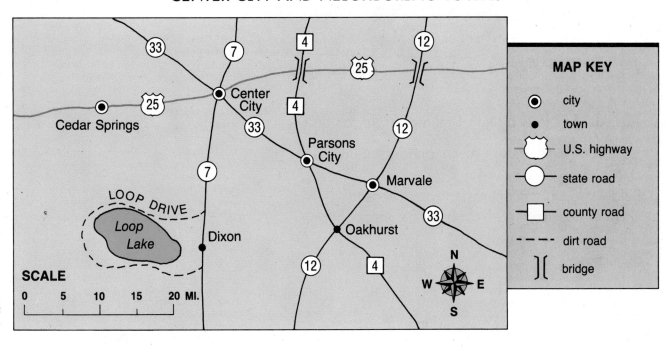

1. Which road goes through Ms. Ford's town? _____

2. Is this a U.S. highway or a state road? _____

3. Does this road go to Oakhurst? _____

4. Ms. Ford drives to Center City from Dixon. Circle the numbers of the routes that go through Center City.

   7   4   33   25

5. Ms. Ford takes Route 33. Will this road take her all the way to Oakhurst? _____

6. Which two roads go through Oakhurst? _____

7. Which route can Ms. Ford take to go straight from Parsons City to Oakhurst? _____

8. How far does Ms. Ford drive from Dixon to Oakhurst? (Remember to use the map scale.) _____

🌐 REVIEW

1. Read each sentence. Put a check (✔) next to each one that is true.

_____ **a.** The difference in size between a large object and its small copy is called a symbol.

_____ **b.** A scale can be shown as a kind of ruler. It can tell how the size of something small compares with something larger.

_____ **c.** The metric system cannot be used to measure distances on a map.

_____ **d.** A mile is a unit of measurement for distance.

_____ **e.** Kilometers are much longer than miles.

2. Below are abbreviations for some measuring units. Draw a line from each word to its abbreviation.

a. inches   cm

b. centimeters   mi.

c. miles   km

d. kilometers   in.

3. Underline the word that best completes each sentence below.

a. Another name for **road** is _____.
scale   distance   route

b. Most main highways have _____ instead of names.
miles   numbers   roads

4. State Highway 100 connects Whiteville and Decaturville in Tennessee. Use the scale to measure the distance between the two towns. It is about _____ miles.
30   60   100

Each year, thousands of people visit a farm near Hodgenville, Kentucky. They go to see a small log cabin. Abraham Lincoln is said to have been born in this house. The road map below shows how to get to Hodgenville and the house. Use it to answer these questions.

1. What symbol on the map stands for Abraham Lincoln's birthplace?

   _____

2. What city is closest to the birthplace?

   _____

3. Which two highways pass through Hodgenville?

   _____   _____

4. Which of these highways is a Kentucky state highway?

   _____

5. Which of these highways goes through several states?

   _____

6. Name a national park on this map.

   _____

7. About how many miles is this park from the Lincoln birthplace?

   _____

8. In what direction is it from the Lincoln birthplace?

   _____

9. There are two ways to get to Mammoth Cave from Hodgenville. Use two different colors to draw each route you could take.

   a. Name the highways in each route.

      Color 1: _____

      Color 2: _____

   b. Which route is shorter? _____

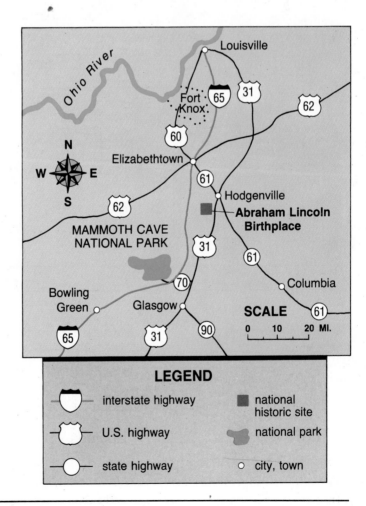

USING A MAP GRID

Some maps have criss-cross lines, something like a big tic-tac-toe drawing. These lines divide the map into squares called a **grid**. The grid helps you find places on a map.

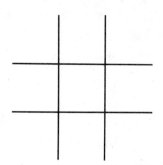

You can see how a grid works by looking below at the picture of a carnival. A set of **letters** goes across the top. A set of **numbers** goes down the side. Suppose you and your friends decide to meet at the carnival at **B-2**. What's there?

Put your finger on **B**. Now move your finger down 2 squares. Is your finger across from the number **2**? You are now in **B-2**. What's there? A merry-go-round! That's where you and your friends will meet.

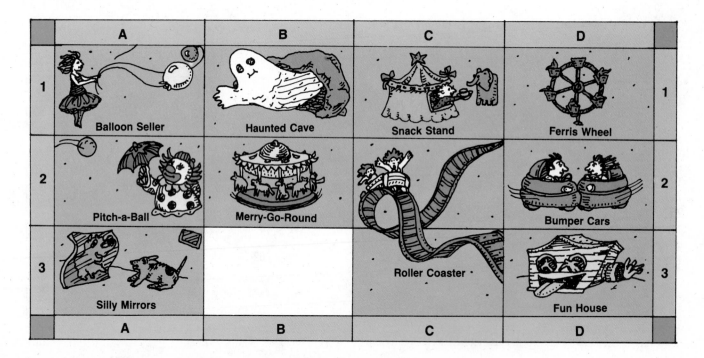

1. Find these squares. Write what you see in them.

   C-1 _____   A-3 _____

2. In which square do you find each of the following? (Give the letter first.)

   Ferris Wheel _____   Haunted Cave _____   Fun House _____

3. In the empty square, draw something for the carnival. What square is it in? _____

Using a map grid . . . on your own

This map shows the state of Iowa. Use the grid to find places.

IOWA

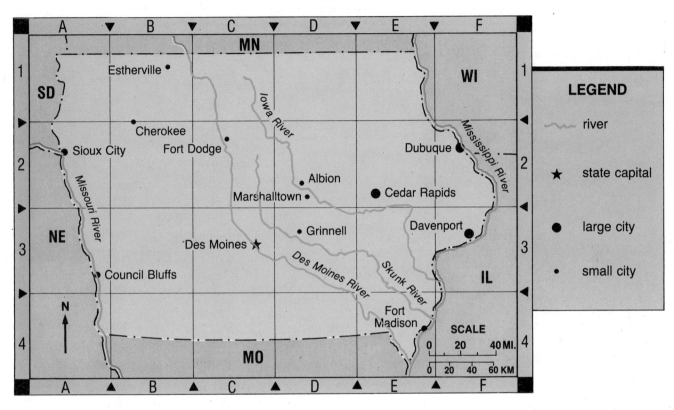

1. Which city do you find in each of the following grid squares?

   B-1 _____   E-2 _____

   A-2 _____   D-3 _____

2. What is the capital of Iowa? _____

3. In which grid square is it located? _____

Underline the word below that completes each sentence correctly.

4. The map shows that Iowa has many _____.   mountains   rivers   valleys

5. The map also shows that many _____ in Iowa
   are located near rivers.   farms   cities   roads

Computer fun

Did you know that pictures for computers and video games are planned on a grid? You can make your own "computer picture" by following the program below. A program is a list of step-by-step instructions that tells the computer exactly what to do. This time, you are the computer.

Just follow each step below. You will see a surprise on the computer screen on page 53.

Step 1: Get a pencil or crayon. Go to step 2.

Step 2: Look at the screen and see how we filled in box A-4. Go to step 3.

Step 3: Fill in boxes B-3, B-5, B-6, B-7, B-8, B-9, B-10, B-11, B-12, B-13. Go to step 4.

Step 4: Fill in boxes C-2, C-13. Go to step 5.

Step 5: Fill in boxes D-1, D-5, D-6, D-13. Go to step 6.

Step 6: Fill in boxes E-1, E-5, E-6, E-10, E-11, E-13. Go to step 7.

Step 7: Fill in boxes F-1, F-10, F-11, F-13. Go to step 8.

Step 8: Fill in boxes G-1, G-8, G-10, G-11, G-13. Go to step 9.

Step 9: Fill in boxes H-1, H-10, H-11, H-13. Go to step 10.

Step 10: Fill in Boxes I-1, I-5, I-6, I-10, I-11, I-13. Go to step 11.

Step 11: Fill in boxes J-1, J-5, J-6, J-13. Go to step 12.

Step 12: Fill in boxes K-2, K-13. Go to step 13.

Step 13: Fill in boxes L-3, L-5, L-6, L-7, L-8, L-9, L-10, L-11, L-12, L-13. Go to step 14.

Step 14: Fill in box M-4. Go to step 15.

Step 15: Read the question under the computer screen. Write the answer on the line.

Step 16: Stop.

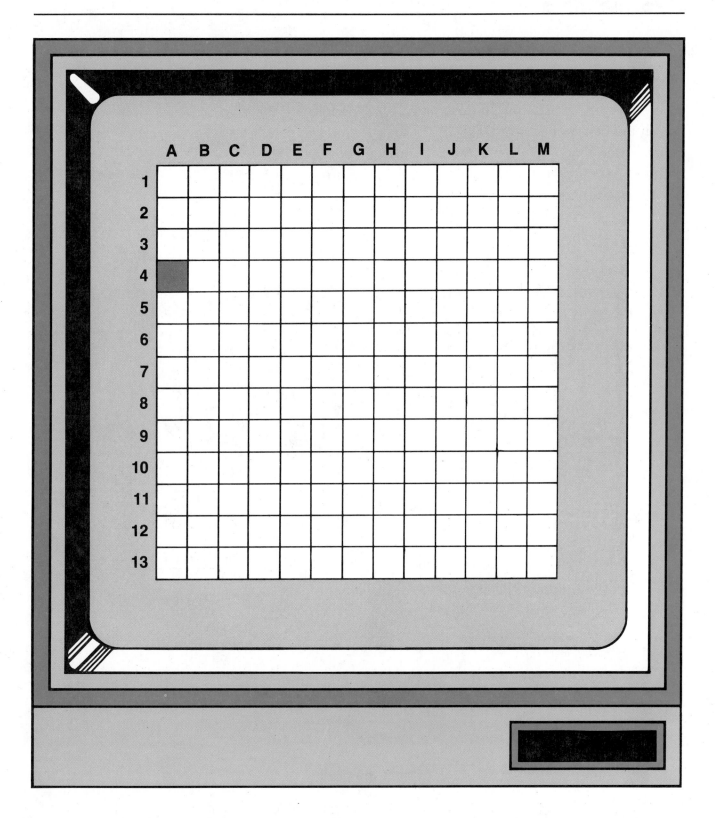

What appeared on the computer screen? _____

SPECIAL PURPOSE MAPS

Some maps give us special information about places.
These kinds of maps are called **special purpose** maps.

Here's one kind of **special purpose map.** Most people see it every
day in the newspaper or on TV. It is a **temperature** map. On the
map, **patterns** and **colors** are used to show temperature in
different parts of the United States. The temperatures on this map
are for a day in early November.

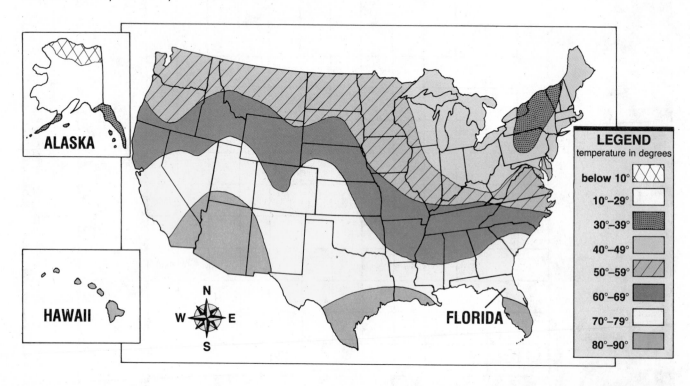

Look at the map. Put a (✓) next to each correct sentence below.

_____ 1. The striped pattern stands for temperatures from 50°–59°.

_____ 2. Alaska had the coldest temperatures on this November day.

_____ 3. Florida was the warmest state on this day.

_____ 4. The temperature for most of the country was above 70°.

_____ 5. The northeast U.S. was colder than the northwest.

_____ 6. If you were on vacation in the southwest on this day,
you'd be in one of the warmest parts of the country.

Practice with a special purpose map

The purpose of this map is to show you where certain animals migrate. Each year, millions of animals migrate, or travel, to and from different places as seasons change. For example, in the fall, many animals migrate south to warm places.

FALL MIGRATION PATHS

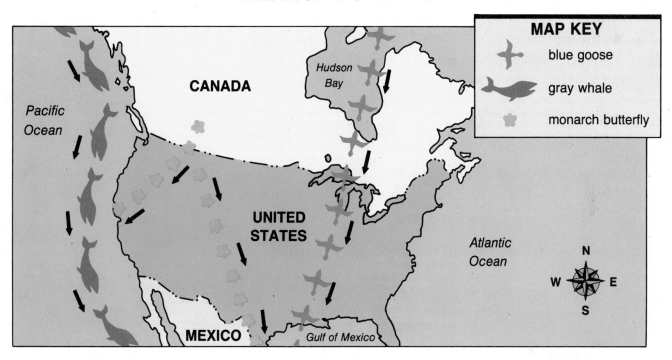

Look at the map to answer the questions below.

1. What three kinds of animals does this map tell you about?

_____   _____   _____

2. a. From which country do the blue geese migrate?   _____

    b. In which direction do they fly in the fall?   _____

3. Some monarch butterflies migrate to California. Where do others migrate?   _____

4. a. In which ocean do the gray whales migrate?   _____

    b. Near which country do they spend the winter?   _____

Using more than one special purpose map

Sometimes you can **put information together** from two maps of the same place. Then you learn more about that place. For example, look at the two maps of the state of Maine, on page 57.

Map A is a **population map.** It shows where people live. Why do more people live in some parts of the state than live in other parts? **Map B** gives you some clues. It shows **highland** and **lowland areas** in Maine. On what kinds of land in Maine do most people live?

1. **a.** On **Map A,** put a check (✔) on the areas in Maine where most people live.

   b. Put an ✕ on the two areas where the fewest people live.

2. **a.** On **Map B,** put a check (✔) on the area of plains.

   b. Put an ✕ on the areas of mountains and highlands.

3. Now look at both **Map A** and **Map B.**

   a. Are any checks in almost the same place on both maps? _____

   b. Are any ✕'s in almost the same place on both maps? _____

Now study **both maps** as you work on page 57.

THE STATE OF MAINE

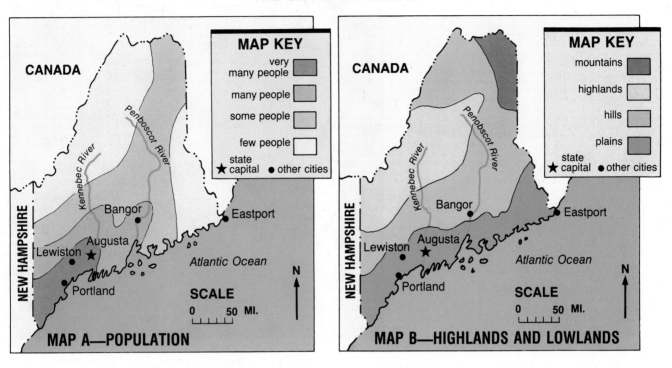

Underline the best answer for items **1–4** below.

1. **Plains** are the same as _____.

   high places   sandy beaches   low, flat lands

2. Few people live in the northwest part of Maine.
   You can guess one reason is that there are many _____.

   highlands   beaches   animals

3. In what kind of land are the large cities located?

   rocky mountains   high plateaus   plains near the coast

Write your answer to the question below.

4. Why do you think most people in Maine live in the southwestern
   part of the state?

   _____

   _____

WE LIVE IN SPACE

Do you have a **globe** in your classroom? A globe is a model of our planet, Earth. Earth is shaped like a ball. So is a globe. A globe shows the **true shapes** and **positions** of all the continents and oceans on Earth.

Today we have a good idea of what our planet looks like. That's because many photos of Earth have been taken from spacecraft. At the right is a photo of Earth taken thousands of miles out in space. You can see certain land and ocean areas. Other parts are hidden by the clouds.

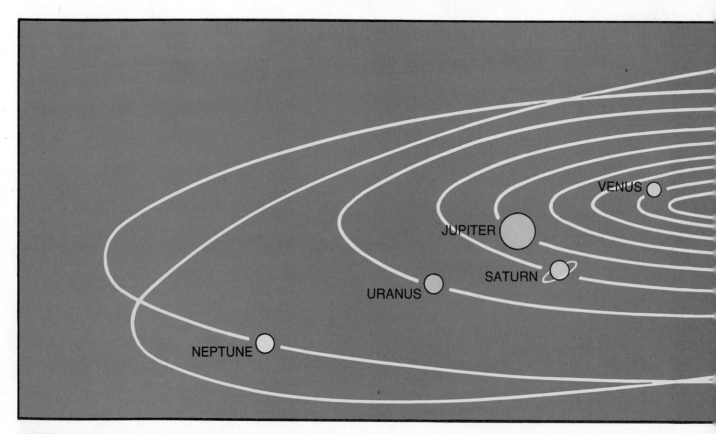

The Sky Map on pages 58–59, shows Earth and the other planets that go around our sun. The sun and its planets are called the **solar system.** The curved lines show the orbits, or paths, that these planets take around the sun. The sun is really much larger than the planets. In this drawing there is not enough room to show its true size compared to the planets.

1. Draw a circle around our planet in the map below.

2. Count the number of planets in our solar system. How many are there? _____

3. Which planet is nearest the sun? _____

4. Is Earth the second or third planet from the sun? _____

5. Name the two planets nearest to Earth. _____ _____

6. Which planet in our solar system do you think is the hottest? _____

   Why? _____

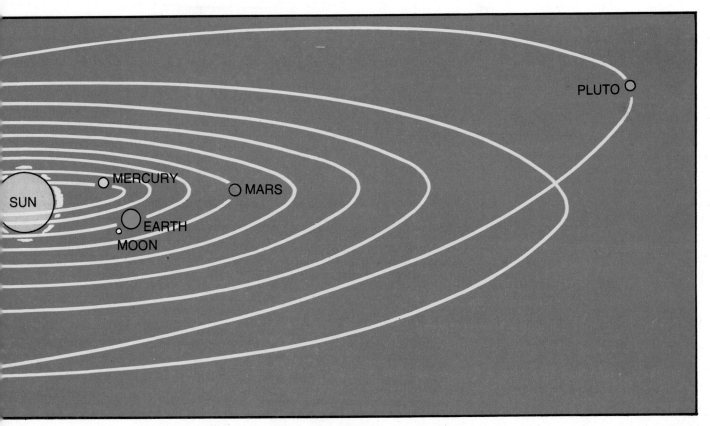

NORTH POLE AND SOUTH POLE

When you see a compass rose on a map, an arrow points **north**. But what is it pointing to? It is pointing in the direction of the **North Pole**.

You can see the North Pole on a globe. It marks the spot that is **farthest north** in the world. When you walk north, you are walking toward the North Pole! To your **right** is **east**. To your **left** is **west**.

The **South Pole** is opposite the North Pole. It marks the spot that is **farthest south** in the world. When you go south, you are going toward the South Pole!

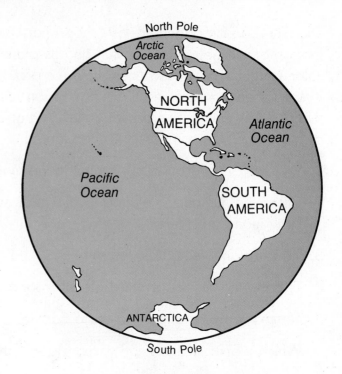

1. The drawings on this page show two sides of a globe. On each one, circle the North Pole. Underline the South Pole.

2. Find the continent of North America. Color it green.

3. The bottom globe has arrows with letters on them. The arrows point in different directions—north, south, east, and west. On the lines below, write the direction in which each arrow points.

A. _____   E. _____

B. _____   F. _____

C. _____   G. _____

D. _____   H. _____

Dividing the globe

Halfway between the North Pole and the South Pole there is a special line drawn by mapmakers. It is called the **equator.** The equator divides the globe into two equal parts called **hemispheres.** The part that contains the **North Pole** is called the **Northern Hemisphere.** The part that contains the **South Pole** is called the **Southern Hemisphere.**

Look at the globes below. On each one, put a ✔ on the **equator.** Study the globes as you answer the questions below.

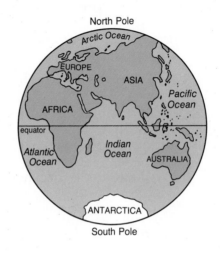

1. Which continents does the equator pass through? _____

2. In which hemisphere is North America located? _____

3. Which hemisphere contains the South Pole? _____

4. In which hemisphere is the continent of Antarctica? _____

5. In which hemisphere is the Arctic Ocean? _____

6. Suppose you took a trip from Australia to Europe.

    a. In which direction would you be going? _____

    b. Which hemisphere would you be coming from? _____

    c. Which hemisphere would you be going to? _____

    d. Would you cross the equator? _____

REVIEW

Look at the maps on page 63 and do the work below.

Write the letters of the map or maps that would help you find:

_____ 1. which U.S. states have alligators.

_____ 2. some main roads in Puerto Rico.

_____ 3. the location of the world's continents.

_____ 4. which continents are crossed by the equator.

_____ 5. the distances between places.

Underline the word that finishes each sentence correctly.

6. The states with alligators are all near _____.   mountains   water   islands

7. Hawaii is made up of eight _____.   peninsulas   islands   states

8. Map E shows that Puerto Rico has many _____.   mountains   lakes   rivers

9. The equator crosses the continents of Africa and _____.

   North America   **Asia**   **South America**

Write the correct word in each blank.
Choose them from the word box.

| Highway 2 | Highway 10 | 60 miles | 47 miles | Pacific |
| Atlantic | Honolulu | Texas | four | five |

10. Hawaii is in the _____ Ocean.

11. In Puerto Rico, _____ is the shortest road
    from Arecibo to Ponce.

12. The capital city of Hawaii is _____.

13. Georgia is bordered by _____ (number) states.

14. The distance from San Juan to Ponce is about _____.

15. The westernmost state with alligators is _____.

MAP A

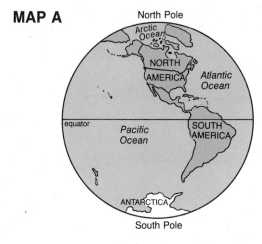

MAP B

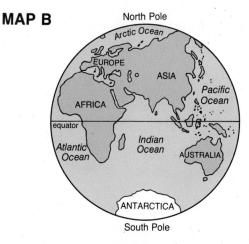

MAP C — WHERE U.S. ALLIGATORS ARE FOUND

OK, AR, TN, NC, MS, SC, AL, GA, TX, LA, FL

Atlantic Ocean

Gulf of Mexico

N
W — E
S

MAP KEY

areas where alligators are found

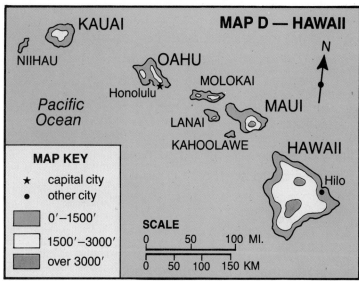

MAP D — HAWAII

KAUAI
NIIHAU
OAHU
Honolulu
MOLOKAI
LANAI
MAUI
KAHOOLAWE
HAWAII
Hilo

Pacific Ocean

N

MAP KEY

★ capital city
● other city
0'–1500'
1500'–3000'
over 3000'

SCALE

0   50   100 MI.

0   50   100   150 KM

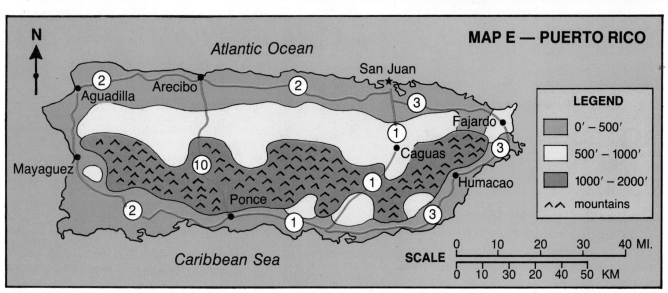

MAP E — PUERTO RICO

N

Atlantic Ocean

Aguadilla, Arecibo, San Juan, Fajardo, Mayaguez, Caguas, Humacao, Ponce

Caribbean Sea

LEGEND

0' – 500'
500' – 1000'
1000' – 2000'
∧∧ mountains

SCALE

0   10   20   30   40 MI.

0   10   30   20   40   50 KM

63

WORDS TO KNOW

borders, boundaries—lines drawn on maps to separate places.

capital—the city where government leaders meet to make the laws of a state or country.

coast, shore—a place where land and water meet.

compass rose—a drawing (like a compass) on a map that shows directions.

continents—the seven largest bodies of land on Earth. They are North America, South America, Asia, Europe, Africa, Australia, and Antarctica.

direction—the way toward or away from a place. The four main directions are north, south, east, and west.

equator—an imaginary line drawn on maps and globes halfway between the North Pole and the South Pole. It divides Earth into northern and southern hemispheres.

globe—a ball-shaped map or model of Earth.

grid—lines drawn on a map that form squares to help you locate places.

hemisphere—half of Earth. The equator divides the globe into the Northern and Southern hemispheres.

island—a body of land with water all around it.

landmark—an object or building that is easily seen. It can help travelers know if they are on the right road.

legend—a list of symbols on a map and what they stand for. It is also called a map key.

map—a drawing of Earth or any place on it. There are also maps of our solar system.

North Pole—the point farthest north on Earth.

ocean—one of the four largest bodies of water on Earth. They are the Atlantic, Pacific, Arctic, and Indian oceans.

peninsula—an area of land with water on three sides.

plain—a wide, flat stretch of land.

plateau—flat land that is higher than the land around it.

route—the road or path going from one place to another.

scale—a measurement that shows how size or distance on a map compares with real size or distance on Earth.

South Pole—the point farthest south on Earth.

solar system—the sun and everything that moves around it. Our solar system has nine planets. The planet we live on is Earth.